SOON AS I GET HOME

SOON AS I GET HOME

BY

DIANA L. LEWIS

© 2016 by Diana L. Lewis

All Rights Reserved. No part of this publication may be reproduced in any form or by any means, including scanning, photocopying, or otherwise without prior written permission of the copyright holder.

Cover illustration by Adrian Lewis

ISBN 978-0-692-82373-6

Contents

Acknowledgements .... *vii*

Chapter 1 .... *1*
   Singing in the rain… *1*
   In the beginning………………... .... *3*
   Mother and daughter love…. *12*
   Maw Maw Love… *16*

Chapter 2 .... *21*
   Family with an "F" *21*
   The Jackson 5-Fan for life *28*
   The House on Adams Street *32*
   College days are here again! *36*

Chapter 3 .... *45*
   Back to the scene of the crime… *45*
   To God be the glory! *55*
   Deep Down….. .... *60*
   Post Acknowledgements *69*

Acknowledgements

First and foremost, the highest praise and acknowledgement that I can give is to my one and only Father up above, God. He has comforted, guided, and loved on me in so many various ways. I finally selected the right fork in the road. What a journey!

Much love and appreciation to the following family and friends:

Adrian Lewis

Jeremy L. Younger, Jonathan S. Lewis, Joshua I. Lewis, Jordan A. Lewis

Ada V. Younger

Jerol L. Younger, Sr.

Jerol L. Younger, Jr (posthumously)

LaDonna K. Younger

Antonia M. King

Kasandra E. Robinson

My precious grandbabies Michael, Jada, Javon, Jodie, Zedekiah, and Zerenity.

Precious Bivings

Mrs. Marvina "Cooky" Levy

Ms. Marsha K. Hardeman

Mrs. Debbie Johnson

Pastor and Mrs. Dennis Dunn

Ms. Lillian Harris

Ms. Vanessa Irizarry

So many more have been a part of my life and I love you all!!

Chapter 1

"Life is not about waiting for the storm to pass, it's about learning to dance in the rain"

Vivian Greene

Singing in the rain...

So here I am. Where am I? What the hell am I doing here? Why the hell am I here? At this point in my life, why am I not further? Why am I at this point and have no purpose? Who in the hell would want to be me? Congestive Heart Failure, Pulmonary Hypertension, Hypertension, Diabetes 2, Osteoarthritis with Degenerative Disc Disease, Obstructive Sleep Apnea, Thyroid Nodules, GERD, Bipolar Disease and Lord knows what the hell else. I have been on oxygen treatment for a number of years, since 2012 with no concrete diagnosis, 16 to 20 pills taken daily and not sure if they are making me better or worse, and uncertainty about seeing the light rays the next morning. Who could pray to be me right now? Nobody

Why Lord? I really don't understand? What have I done in my life that warrants my life to be in this sort of fix? I know that I have not done my best. I realize that I have sinned often. Yet, I have asked God to forgive me many times. I don't expect God to forgive me for it all, but I am praying that He will take it into consideration. Is this punishment for my past behaviors? If so, then I understand. However, I often wonder, where are the punishments for those that have hurt me emotionally and physically? Why are some of them reaping benefits and enjoying their lives, while I continue to suffer? Laying on a sick bed, struggling to survive?

My story does not begin here. This is a synopsis of my current situation. It has taken me many years to write this story. It has been painful for me. However, I am ready and willing to tell the story in its entirety. It has conjured up a lot of old feelings that may send me into a dark place that I prefer not to be. I promise to take my time and ease you through my journey to finding my way home. It took me 32 years to decide to compose this and want to make it well worth it. I take all these pains to blast painful memories, memories that should never raise their ugly heads again, memories that, once thought of, give me a source of sorrow, heart breaks and regrets.

Praying for God to lead and guide me through this journey that I have wanted to travel for a long time. So here we go, brace yourselves for a long journey back in time.

In advance, I will say, that there may be people that will be upset emotionally by the things that may be stated. I won't apologize for this because these are my true recollections and remembrances of the incidents that have occurred. If you were involved and are hurt, God is ready for you to repent. No need to apologize to me, give it to the Father. He will take care of you. I have already been damaged by your actions, no need to apologize. In turn, if I have done anything that may have hurt anyone I ask for forgiveness for my actions. In the end, we will get through it all! This is my platform in which to get through it and survive. Please know that because of the deliberate actions of others it has not only caused difficulties in my life, but the lives of my children, grandchildren and those that love me dearly, because I am unable to give my all! It all snowballs and is not pretty. It is devastating indeed! I thank God for where I am now. He has brought me thus far. Nobody has been there for me, but God!

Okay, so enough of the preface. Can you tell that I am holding back? Is it time? I suppose so. Let's go girl! Hold me Lord!

In the beginning.........

My mother, father and I were living in a small single room shack in Spencer, Oklahoma. My parents were very young and at the ages of 15 and 17, I was born. I was the first-born child of five kids. My parents threw themselves into an adult situation, which back then in the 1960's was not really unheard of, but yet, still frowned upon. But, "If you make your bed you will have to lie in it". This was a phrase that my mother, my mother's mother and so on used. Often, it is also a phrase that I use even now with my sons. I never really knew what it meant until I got into my older and mature years. Laughable, isn't it? Am I at that point in my life now? It's really questionable. Sometimes, I feel like I'm a young child. At times, I feel as though I have multiple personalities. Actually, I'm beginning to think that I have more and more personalities that I never knew about, there is still more to me than I know about. So, since we are discussing multiple personalities, here are mine:

1. Diana-The childlike princess
2. Diana-Ms. Sophisticated (Diva Di, Lady Di)
3. Diana-Bad "B" (angry, rebellious)
4. Diana-Compassionate, Loving, Caring to all
5. Diana-Scared and Frightened
6. Diana-Ms. Educated (I know everything)

I've gone off into a bi-polar moment. Or maybe this is truly just me in my entirety. God help me.

So, imagine a young girl living in a world all of her own. A world in which she believes everyone should be kind, loving and compassionate to all, a world whereby, all that happens is good, and good alone, with no incidence of hurt, that there should be no hurt, harm or pain. But, unfortunately for her hurt, harm and pain is a true reality.

This was a little girl that was so frightened, so afraid and unsure of what was to happen next. Unsure of the darkness, she often longed for the light. So frightened when nights came because of the thoughts of the awful things that would happen at night. Anger, abuse, alcoholic screams and yells would permeate the house throughout the night. She was so scared. Why God? Why did she have to experience this? She wanted to live the dream life of a princess. A perfect, shiny and bright life. She wanted to live a life in which everyone loved one another. Everyone cared and took care of each other. Why was she so naïve? What was wrong with her?

So, my father and mother lived in the rural area of Spencer, Oklahoma in a small, one room shack. I remember my parents saying that they would place me in a chest of drawers, because they did not have a crib or bassinet for me. They were young, black, and with no forms of financial means other than the side jobs my father performed. My grandparents would help with the purchase of milk, diapers and caring for me on many occasions.

I remember my first day of kindergarten at Parker Elementary in Spencer, Oklahoma. My mother had dressed me up and prepared me for my first day of school. I was very scared when my mother dropped me off, but eventually became comfortable as the day went on and I was able to become accustomed to the structured environment. As time went on, I enjoyed the school environment more than I did at home. This was because I found more peace within the school walls for the few hours of being within it, than I have ever found at home.

I remember one day walking home from school in the rain, and it was very muddy. I had learned to walk home from school by myself. I had to get used to it since no one came to get me after school hours. I remember slipping and falling in the mud. My clothes became extremely muddy and one of my shoes got stuck and came off! I cried so, because I hurt my knees. I was also very dirty and muddy, and I also knew that I was going to get into a lot of trouble. At that point, I felt alone, defeated and ugly all at the same time. No one came to my aid, it really felt bad having the feeling that no one cared.

My mother would always dress me well and she took great pride in it. She would always comb and hot press my hair with expertise. She always made sure that I looked my very best. That was one of the things that I loved so much about my mother.

My father was in and out of our lives. When he was there, he was an awesome provider. However, anger, alcohol, and adultery seemed to matter most in his life. At that time my father seemed to be depressed about his life, past and present. He loved his family; I believe but did not know how to take care of us, because of his broken and damaged past. He was a man that allowed his past to get in the way of his love for us.

He was an angry young man and it showed through the physical violence that was placed upon my mother often. I remember hearing my mother screaming and crying as he dragged her around the house or sometimes outside on the sidewalk. Those vicious events would often occur after my father had been out drinking and being with other women. I believe that because of his guilt, he would bring his insecurities, past horrors, hatred for enemies, inability to be a responsible father, loving husband and place all of this on my mother in the form of vicious slaps and degrading language.

Because of my father's behavior, my mother would in turn reciprocate her anger toward me. At one point, I thought that my mother truly despised me. I could see the hatred in her eyes every time that she disciplined me. I never knew that anyone could hate someone that much, especially since I wasn't sure as to why I was being disliked, and when you are sure that what you did does not warrant much punishment, if any at all. It was truly perplexing to me and remained that way for many years.

I wasn't sure of the cycle of destruction that was permeating throughout my life, but it was definitely destroying lives left and right. It was not healthy for any child to grow up in this stage. I felt more like I was in prison rather than being home, so you could imagine what I went through.

My parents were two persons totally unequally yoked. Two individuals from two totally different backgrounds that came together because of extenuating circumstances, set up a life of destruction, unknowingly, for themselves and the children that they birthed in to this horrifically, sinful world. They did not feel it as much as we did, because we experienced the anger from them first hand, and never felt comfortable being with our parents, one minute we are all sitting, enjoying quietness while it lasts, the next minute, chaos would erupt and the vicious cycle would begin all over again.

Five precious angels were born from this mismatched gathering. We were four beautiful girls and one handsome dude. There was also one boy that was still born, my brother, Rodney Lyn Edward Younger. Due to my father's continued philandering he helped to reproduce another son with another woman. Till this day, my father has no knowledge of this son's whereabouts, name or anything about him. So, I have a half-brother that I have no idea who and where he is. I hope to find him one day. I'm determined. And I hope he does not suffer the same fate as me and my siblings, me especially.

I sometimes wonder if my father feels any guilt or shame from the irresponsible actions that he has performed and the outcomes that have resulted from them. Outcomes that have inadvertently reaped a huge amount of hurt and pain on so many. I have always wondered that the reason for my dad's drinking and physical abuse of my mother was because of his deep hurts and pain and his inability to refrain from it. So, his preference was to wallow in it and cover his hurts with alcohol which barely had any positive results, but rather, made him a very sad and depressed man.

I understand that my father was raised by his grandmother and grandfather. His mother was in and out of his life and he did not know who his biological father was until he became older. So, my father's life had been set up for failure before he was able to speak. His grandparents raised him and did all they knew how to. Chaos, drinking, shooting, fighting and womanizing were all that he knew. It was no wonder that things turned out the way in which they did. He was trained that way, and there was very little anyone could do about that.

Growing up and learning about my grandparents, I blamed them more about our father's misfortunes, but as time rolled by, I realized the real cause of his misfortunes was himself, and his inability to refrain from dwelling in the past, it was his choice to live like that.

I felt sorry for my dad at times because of the difficulties that he had endured, and the fact that he did not know who his father was; he truly had a right to feel worthless and unloved. I imagine that he felt he was not worthy of being loved or cared for. He was so wrong on all levels. We loved our dad and would have loved to have seen more of him. However, his alcohol was much more important than we were at the time. It was often reflected in how he treated us in comparison with his bottles. He once beat my mother up for purchasing new furniture to make the house look nice and as usual, she vented the anger on me.

I do remember those times when he would come home and cook food and pass out, forgetting that the food he had put on the stove was still cooking and cause a fire on the stove. There were times that I woke up to smoke coming from the kitchen while sleeping in the living room on the sofa. The outcome could have been much worse but God covered and protected us all.

I at that time, being so young did not know that much about God. We hadn't really been introduced to God, because we hadn't really been to church. Later on, however, my mother would have the Sunday school bus pick us up and take us to church.

I loved going to church, singing songs, listening to the pastor speak. Church was a way for me to get away from the physical and emotional abuse that was being felt on a day to day basis. The mother's and deacons at the church were firm, yet kind and I appreciated it. In going to church, I was getting to know more about God, Jesus and the Holy Spirit. It was a way for me to place myself into another world that was much more peaceful than the one I had been currently placed in. In a nutshell,

I found succor at church after the trauma I must have faced at home.

There were portions of my childhood that I have blocked out and am totally unable to remember. I'm not sure why I can't remember. I figure it's because the memories are all too traumatic and my mind may have just shut down.

So, my memory now takes me to living in Oklahoma City, Oklahoma as a young child. I truly loved my siblings and still do, although one of us is missing from the group now. That is another chapter that will be discussed later on.

We had a good relationship between us despite all that was going on around us. We loved playing together and played the typical childhood games. We were also very protective of one another and when something happened to one of us, the older siblings would go and handle the situation. I as the oldest generally was the one who was ready to protect my siblings, always. Even as an adult I found myself being very protective of my sisters with their boyfriends or husbands etc. We continue to have that protective relationship now. However, I tend to use diplomacy in handling difficult situations regarding my sisters; I learned to keep myself out of their private lives.

"First my Mother forever my Friend"

Mother and daughter love....

My mother and I had a very tumultuous relationship and as the oldest child, I experienced and saw a lot of my mother and father's physical and emotional disagreements.

I felt bad for my mom and really despised my father at that time. My mother worked hard to take care of us. She worked hard to decorate the house and keep it neat, clean and orderly. Whatever my father had dealt with out on the streets he brought it home and subjected my mother to it. He obviously wasn't fully aware that he was subjecting us to the madness from out on the streets as well as what happened inside the house too.

There were times when I would cry silently as I sat huddled behind my bedroom door, or sometimes in the bathroom listening and wishing for it all to end. I didn't know a lot about God or praying, other than what I had been taught at church, so I would just cry out for it all to stop and quickly!

Eventually, the fighting would stop and it would become quiet again. I listened to make sure that my mother was okay. I could hear her whimpers and shifting around picking up the house. My dad would usually leave out and go wherever he would venture after each violent incident. He would be gone for a number of days, then return as if nothing had transpired.

I never understood how he could return and want to start the process all over again, knowing that eventually the situation would just reoccur again, a vicious cycle that seemed like a never ending series. I wondered how he never got tired of the same routine as mom obviously got tired of the whole situation, so did we.

As I became older, we would receive calls from a few of my father's other women. They didn't seem to have any shame at all. Sometimes my mother would catch the phone before one of us could. Somehow, I could sense that my mother's feelings were hurt, even though I didn't know very much about what it meant to have an adult relationship and to be hurt so many times. I would pick up the phone and tell them not to call ever again! What an awful mess for a child to have to experience, and endure.

My mother birthed me when she was 15 years old. What a life, raising five children, dealing with a spouse that drank, was a womanizer and not seeming to want a better life for himself or anyone else was quite a heavy load to bear. Yet it was the one that was chosen for her at that particular time.

Now, please don't get me wrong, I do want to clarify that I love both of my parents dearly; however, it is what it is. This is my memoir and my recollection of my life. This is therapy for me. I need and have to release a lot of this in order to move on and live. Life is about moving forward, moving closer to God, and more toward His love and word. That is my focus at this present time in my life.

There were times my mother would take us with her to run errands, go shopping and visit friends and family. Because there were five of us, we would sometimes have to stay in the car. I hated going anywhere because of this. The fact that we would have to stay in the car for it seemed like hours. Whether it was going to Target, Woolworth or TG&Y we would sit and wait. I could never understand why my mother would leave us in the car and not even come back to check on us. No water, treats or anything while we waited. My siblings would be restless, yelling, fighting amongst themselves as I tried to calm them down. I didn't want to get into trouble with my mother if they got out of the car. So we would wait and when she did return she would bring a treat or something for us.

At times when we would go to friends or family's houses we would again sometime have to sit in the car or sit and wait inside their homes afraid to move, or take the chance of being disciplined.

I feared my mother a lot, and she made sure of that. There was something about the anger in her face and her voice that caused me to feel unsure and unloved. I tried often to get my mother to love me and to show her love, by a simple hug or gesture. I longed at times for a gentle hug or a simple "I love you" or "It's going to be alright". But unfortunately, I never received it. I strongly believe that because my mother was broken in so many areas that she didn't have the ability to accept, show or receive love because she had never received it herself. Even today, I seek it, but not as much as I did at that time. Now again, don't misinterpret my love for my mother. I love my mother dearly. It is her behavior that I didn't like at times. I still have a problem with it, but its better. I guess because I am older and more tolerable it doesn't bother me as much.

I remember sometimes my mother would buy special treats for her and for us, which wouldn't last long being that there were 5 of us. Anyway, she would hide her treats and we would sneak into her room, find her treats and take a little out. We tried our best to make sure that it wasn't noticeable. But, she would always notice and someone would get in to trouble. And most of the time it was always me, as she felt I taught my siblings the act of stealing the treats. At times, my treats were forcefully forfeited as punishments and shared among my siblings.

No kid would have envied my life, not in any bit, as I never enjoyed anything most average kids enjoy; both motherly and fatherly care and love, a good night's rest, and twenty-four hours without receiving as little as a slap. No kid obviously wants to be deprived of these.

I hated my life as a child. There were many times that I would create my own fairytale world. This was the only way for me to take myself from the life that I was being held captivate in. I at times didn't know if I would ever make it through! Things seemed so difficult. But somehow, I knew that God would bring me out, when and at what time I wasn't sure, but I know it had to happen and soon.

So, I don't know quite where I left off, besides the fact that I am all over the place with this life story. The reason I am all over the place is because I felt as though my life was all over the place at the time.

Maw Maw Love...

My paternal grandmother, whom I loved so much, was called "Maw Maw". All of the grandchildren called her this and they all loved her dearly. We always looked forward to visiting with her and sleeping over. There were many, many times that we were not allowed to go and spend the night with her, no matter how much we would ask. My mother was very protective of us and did not trust the environment that my grandmother lived in. This was added to the fact that she had trust issues due to the circumstances that surrounded her. Plus, I don't think that she believed that we were being supervised very well. I think that she believed that we pretty much were taking care of ourselves, because my grandmother was so sick and spent most of her time in her lounge chair, sofa or bed. She was pretty much correct. I was the oldest and helped to oversee everyone. We were allowed to stay overnight one night and our parents would come to pick us up the next night. It wasn't that we were allowed to stay often, but when we were, we had so much fun!

My grandmother was lovable, kind and endearing and she loved each and every one of her grandchildren. She was sick, had heart disease and was unable to physically enjoy time with us. She had to take nitroglycerin tablets often when she had chest pain. I still remember when she would call for one of us to bring her "nitro" drugs for her in her squeaky old voice.

She loved to eat and would treat us to delicacies like: fried chicken, buttermilk and cornbread, and candy treats. Sometimes she would send us down to the corner café in the 5 points area of Denver, Colorado to get her two pig ears sandwiches and foot long chili hot dogs for each of us. We were usually overjoyed at this offer as we often ran down to the café.

I remember walking down the dark rural city streets with my brother holding the money tight in my hand. I would be so scared that someone would jump out and attack us at any moment. The 5 points area was a rural area in which there was a lot of rundown buildings at the time, unkempt homes and yards, not desirable living at that time. My grandmother lived in a building that was called "The White Palace". There actually was a point and time in which our family lived in that very same building. In fact, I solicited my first job there, sweeping and vacuuming hallway floors. The manager of the building would pay me a couple of dollars a week to do this. It was a joy for me and allowed for me to have my own money.

So, once we reached the café, bought our food and returned to my grandmother's apartment we felt much better.

I was so unaware of the fact that God was carrying us from the apartment to the café with His Heavenly Angels guiding us all the way through. My grandmother was always excited when we returned with the food and lovingly watched as we passed the food out and gave her the pig ear sandwiches she had requested. We would all sit and eat watching one of our favorite television programs.

My grandmother taught me how to crochet and knit. She taught me how to make scarves, blankets and caps. She also taught me how to figure out crosswords and word search puzzles. I so enjoyed these special times we spent with her. She was so genuine and kind to all of her grandchildren and we all loved her. I enjoyed my best years with her as there were usually no insecurities when we were with her. I hardly thought of home when I was with grandma.

I was devastated, when in 1981 she passed away while I was in my freshman year of college, due to complications from a bypass surgery. My grandmother had such a difficult time eating healthy. She smoked profusely and did not exercise, all against doctor's requests. But during that time she didn't know. And I don't think she really cared. She just enjoyed life and that was all. She had a popular saying about "Living life like it's your last day on earth". She always seemed happy, and I miss her smile, even till today.

I remember speaking to her on the phone a couple of days before I was to go to college. I was at my mom's beauty salon getting my hair done for my first day of college. I remember as though it was yesterday. I told her that I wanted to see her again and she said "Okay baby, see you soon". Many months after that, she passed away. I remember crying profusely not only about her passing, but the fact that I never was able to tell her good bye! Why didn't God allow me to say my parting words to someone who was so near and dear to my heart? Despite all of the dysfunctional people in my family why did she have to be the one to go?

My grandmother's funeral was quite sad of course. I was asked to sing at the funeral and there was a discussion as to what I was to sing. I was asked to sing something up tempo nothing slow. But in the end, I ended up singing the ballad that I had planned to sing in the beginning. It was much too stressful a time to be worried about anything else.

Afterwards, we returned home by airplane, which was funded by my college funds, of which was never replaced back into my financial aid account, but had been promised that it would be. The financial advisor had specifically informed us that it would need to be replaced back into my account. I, however, never realized it and ended up with a deficit in my account the following school year that I couldn't repay. That marked the end of course of my college career. No one of course took it into consideration, nor did they care. Why was I surprised?

Chapter 2

"Family, like branches on a tree, we all grow in different directions, yet our roots remain as one"

Blog post by A Place for Mom

Family with an "F"

There were many times that it felt like our family was much more than the norm. That dysfunctionality was not the primary adjective. As a family, we did love being with one another. We loved to go on family gatherings when finances permitted. There were times when we would go on family outings to McDonalds on Fridays. I really enjoyed when my dad would get off of work and take us to McDonalds for a happy meal for each and every one of us. As a child that was the highlight of my day.

My dad loved to go fishing and we loved going with him, hanging out by the river, sitting on a blanket and eating fried chicken and potato salad that my mom had cooked. My dad would usually catch a number of fish and he taught me how to clean the fish for cooking. Those days of happiness were really special for me and my siblings. My dad would be in a good mood and so would my mother.

However, as soon as we would get home, finish our meals and go to bed I would hear my mother screaming, my dad yelling and the sound of breaking dishes, loud crashing, and total chaos. I would go to my closed door and listen, feeling so helpless. I felt so bad for my mother and hated my dad.

Believe it or not, at times I would like it when my father would drink, because he had a false sense of love and was much more likable to us. In addition, he would do more for us when he was drinking. But, by the time the next day would come around he would be irritable, distant and grouchy. I could not understand this illness they called "alcoholism". It was so confusing to me at that time and it still is really.

Because of this disease that my father had for so many years, he was unable to protect me and my siblings. He was unable to protect me from being molested at the age of 10 years old. This portion of my life was one of the most frightening experiences that I had ever had to endure. An experience I would certainly not wish for any child to go through.

In recollection, the pleasant times in my childhood, I would say were those times when I was able to be alone. I always enjoyed playing alone by myself. Although I had 4 other siblings and we had a lot of fun times playing together, I enjoyed playing alone.

So much fun was enjoyed pretending that I had a beautiful home, with the cans, boards and whatever I had to utilize to complete my make shift play area. I was in my own world and was quite territorial about it! I did not want anyone to be a part of it because it was my only sanctuary. And at times it was the only place that I felt safe, away from the alcoholism, the physical and emotional abuse. Away from the dysfunction and confusion. Away from the belittling, hurt, shame, depression, everything! It was my sanctuary and I cherished it. I truly believe that God set that area up for me, as a place of solace, for He knew what I needed. I would sit out there and play all day, talking to myself with my imaginary perfect family. Of course, once my imaginary family would go away, I would have to go right smack back into my true reality.

As I lay in my bed, night slowly turned into day, and my heart would be warm and giddy. This warmth was due to the fact that I had something pleasant to look forward to with my imaginary family. Once I made it through the disturbing unrest of the day and was able to fall back into my imaginary world, everything would be okay.

Even at an early age, I was determined to become employed. I inquired about a program that was in a comic book that required you solicit greeting cards to make extra money. I would walk up and down the rural roads of Spencer, OK soliciting to a number of people that I knew in the neighborhood. I really enjoyed visiting and talking with the residents as it made me feel special. My mother and father were okay with me going door to door soliciting for the greeting cards. They however, advised me to be careful. So there were no issues with that and as I stated I felt good about it.

I loved going to a couple of the elderly women and talking with them about the products that I had. They were kind, firm at times, advising me to be careful walking around the neighborhood alone and would give me cookies and milk as a snack. Sometimes, they would give me pointers on how to solicit my products. I would take the added tips as they were true gems to me.

So, the greeting card business was not profitable for me and I ended up after a couple of months or so putting it to the side. I knew that I would find another project to venture into soon. I still never lost my interest in being employed as it was on my wish list.

In Spencer we lived in another house, it was a brick home with 3 bedrooms, fireplace, an acre or more of rural land in the back and it was quite roomy. My dad would work on fixing it up inside and out. My mother was good with decorating and really should have been an interior decorator. She did an impeccable job decorating our room with beautiful blue stripped wall paper, solid blue curtains, matching rugs, comforters, sheets and twin beds. We really loved our rooms and mother took great pride in decorating them.

I remember once going to the kitchen for water in the middle of the night and seeing what I thought was a black shoe on the living room floor. Now, I knew that if my mother saw that shoe in the living room she was going to be upset! So, I went to pick it up and the shoe moved! The shoe or what I thought was a shoe moved quickly past me! That was when I realized that it wasn't a shoe, but what they called a "wood rat"! A huge black rat that seemed to have moved at top speed across that living room floor! I screamed until my mom and dad came, asked me what was wrong and sent me to bed. I was so scared from that experience that I would not get up in the middle of the night again! Not even to go to the bathroom. It was also, not too soon after that I knew that I needed glasses and so did my mother.

Although she was excellent at keeping her house in order and decorated well, it was not without the assistance that she required from us. I was older, so of course I was expected to perform more chores than the others. I would help my brother and sisters at times to keep them from getting into trouble. But, usually if something did not get completed, I was always the one getting disciplined for everyone's short comings.

Now don't get me wrong, I was never a rebellious child. I always did what I was told and sometimes more. I was a child that would always be there, go the extra mile to help in anything that I was asked to do. I was always willing to please anyone and everyone. I worked especially hard to please my mother. I did everything that I thought that I could to try to make her love me. I felt that because I wasn't doing or being what she wanted me to be that I had to continue to try until I received that acknowledgement. Unfortunately, I am still waiting; the acknowledgements had never come, not even from my siblings that I suffered for at times.

There was a moment in which I really was afraid that I would not make it out of the discourse that I was in. I remember one day that I had wanted to wear a fancy purple skirt or at least I thought that it was fancy. So I rolled the skirt up and changed at school. I felt really good wearing the skirt and was quite proud of myself. The boys seemed to notice me a little and that made me happy, although I didn't have a clue as to what boys were all about, I just knew that I wanted them to notice me. It felt a little pleasing getting attention from the opposite sex.

After school, I got back to the house and was changing my skirt in the bathroom when all of a sudden, my mother came into the bathroom and raised her arm and down came the belt across my leg, arms and back. I remember crawling underneath the sink and crying out from the pain and from the emotional hurt that I felt, because I wasn't sure of why I was being disciplined, especially in this way. I figured out why she was so angry and that was because I had worn the skirt to school without her permission. However, I still don't believe that it was a reason to discipline me in that manner. I was depressed and hurt for a while afterwards. I really felt after that incident that my mother truly did not love me at all.

The next day, I was still pained and my mother acted as if nothing had happened. I could not understand this behavior at all. Of course, I was only 8 or 9 at the time and shouldn't have been expected to understand.

Of course, that was not by far the last severe form of discipline that I received, there were many after that. I was even at times expected to go out to the yard and get switches (thin tree limbs) to be disciplined with. I of course, could not understand that concept. I believe that the emotional abuse was much worse than the physical abuse. However, they both marked me for life or so I thought.

During the time in which we were living in the house I was slowly coming into my depression. I believe I was around the age of 9 years old. I know I was no older than 9 because we moved to Denver, Colorado by the time I was 10 years old and that was when another difficult time of my life transpired. It was the most life changing event in my life. Soon, I will reveal this epic portion of my story.

However, I was really sad, distraught, felt lonely and showed it often. I've always wondered if anyone was aware of the fact that I was sad. Did anyone take a moment in time to give me a hug or ask me if I was okay? Did anyone ever ask me to sit down, talk and discuss the way that I was feeling? There was a picture that shows me on the porch of the house with my mom's arms around me as though all was just perfect. It wasn't for me at the time and if you looked at the picture you could see that I was depressed and very sad. I was feeling so horrible at that time and that also may have been the time that I was coming into adolescence. Whatever the case, my feelings were all over the place.

Still waiting to get home. Where are you Toto?

The Jackson 5-Fan for life

So, there was a time that I believed that my mother was the most wonderful mother in the world when she introduced me to a very talented group of young boys called "The Jackson 5 from Gary, Indiana!"

It was a nice warm day and I had been outside playing in the yard when my mother called me in to see something on the television. There before my eyes I saw a group of handsome young boys singing in harmony, dancing in succession with the smoothest of ease. Standing out in front was a young boy, who was so smooth and entertaining that I thought I would faint. The young man I found out was named Michael. I instantly fell in love with him! At that time they were on the Ed Sullivan Show singing the hit song "ABC". I was glued (literally) to the screen and clapped with glee afterwards. I had never seen anything like that before and was literally flabbergasted. That was one of my first experiences with being infatuated with boys. From that day onwards I became a loyal fan.

I bought every magazine and poster that I could find that had pictures of the Jackson 5. I would place them all over my room walls. Whenever a television program would come on that would feature the Jackson 5 such as: "Sonny and Cher", "American Bandstand", or "The Johnny Carson Show" to name a few, I could not wait to watch it. Sometimes, my brother would fight with me because his football or basketball games would come on at the same time and we would fight over the television. I would win most of the time, but he would win sometimes because my dad would agree with him. This of course would make me so mad that I would go into my room and cry. It was literally like an addiction.

My mother knew that I was a diehard fan, so every Christmas she would purchase for me the new Jackson 5 album or when Michael transitioned from the group to a solo career, she purchased his albums. After the first Christmas, I knew that she would buy me an album each year because I would let her know in advance about the new album coming out. I sometimes in anticipation would sneak around her room to see if she had purchased the new album. And each time I found out that she had purchased it without fail. I truly loved my mother for this!

As an adolescent, I had seen Michael Jackson and the Jackson 5 twice in my lifetime, once in San Francisco, California and as an adult in Denver, Colorado. My mother had set up the San Francisco concert trip for me and my siblings. What an extremely fun time we had! It was a once in a lifetime experience! We were even able to see the Jackson 5's limousine as it pulled off after the concert!

I followed Michael Jackson and the Jackson 5/The Jacksons all through high school and college. Upon hearing of Michael's passing I was completely numbed and in disbelief. At this point, I still haven't come to grips with it. It is a day that will be with me for the rest of my life. The world lost an icon, a legend. Rest in paradise Michael Jackson; King of Pop.

My other joy, which still is pleasant for me now, is my love for music. I have always loved music and I remember as a child that when my mother would leave the house for work or running errands, I would love to go into the living room and listen to her gospel music. At that time I loved listening to the music of Shirley Caesar, The Five Blind Boys, James Cleveland, Walter and Edwin Hawkins and The Love Center Choir, Aretha Franklin, Stevie Wonder, just to name a few. I am almost certain that this is where my musical roots stemmed from. I would turn the music on, sing and hum as though I were performing live on stage. I always envisioned that one day I would sing live in front of a host of people. That one day I would be as famous as Diana Ross or Aretha Franklin wearing beautiful dresses, shoes, hairstyles, makeup. I would be living a lavish lifestyle, in the most beautiful homes and driving the fanciest cars. I had high hopes, but had no idea how to obtain them at all.

At times, I would go to the bathroom to clean up, dress up and make up, then stand in front of the mirror and sing to myself. No one ever really saw me, so I guess that is just our little secret.

I loved singing so much that I would sometimes sing to myself outside or in front of my family. They would always ask me to sing "I'll Be There" by The Jackson 5. It was a favorite song of mine at that time and although I was scared to death I loved singing. My family would ask me and my siblings to get together, pretend we were the Jackson 5 and sing along with the 45rpm record. It was fun, but nerve-racking and I did not like being put on the spot, but had no choice at the time.

Music was another way in which I was able to go into my inner self and feel safe there. No one would hurt me or cause me to feel nervous when I was singing. Well, that is until my mother, father or siblings would walk into the room and interrupt my makeshift concert. And of course that would be that.

My musical endeavors continued throughout my young years while in middle school and high school. I was chosen to participate in all-state choirs, city wide choirs, music camps, talent shows, etc. I remember one incident in particular in which my music teacher in middle school had wanted me to participate in the annual school talent show. She had been working with me on a particular song that she wanted me to perform. Well, I had sang lead vocals with the school choirs and many of the before mentioned choirs, but never completely by myself.

When the day for the program came, I was a complete nervous wreck. My mother promised she would be there, but never showed up. When the time came for me to sing I stepped on stage. For some reason the song was not coming out the way that I had envisioned that it would. All of a sudden, the kids in the audience began to laugh and shout "Boo, Boo!" Well, of course I ran off the stage crying my eyes out. My music teacher tried her best to console me, but it was too late. The damage had already been done. I was seriously traumatized. I didn't know if I would ever recover, or ever want to sing again!

Well of course we see where that story went next! I continued to sing and perform while at the middle school. My music teacher continued to encourage me to sing even more. She saw something within me that I couldn't see at that time. I truly wish that I could remember her name. I would really love to thank her for the encouragement, support and belief in me.

"Childhood Is the Kingdom Where Nobody Dies."
-Edna St. Vincent Millay

The House on Adams Street

There are many, many portions of my life that I cannot seem to remember as I have stated before. I am not quite sure what my mind has blocked and why, but I cannot seem to recover certain times in my life. I can't seem to remember how old I was at the times when my memory had lapsed. I believed that I was in junior high school when we lived in Denver, Colorado. I believe at that time there may have been a traumatic event that happened at that time that caused me to tuck those portions of my life away. Safe from the hurt and harm that I know that they would cause.

There is one memory that I could not forget, that I sometimes wish that I could forget. Something that I wish had never happened because it almost caused me to lose my life more times than I could count.

It was our second trip back to Denver, Colorado, moving from Spencer, Oklahoma. My paternal grandmother had requested that we move back as she wanted her family to be closer to her. My grandmother had married a man that would be my step grandfather. He had been in the U.S. Army during WWII and while in the military had been burned severely over a large percentage of his body. His body was seriously disfigured. But we didn't care about that, we loved him and thought the world of him. All the grandkids called him "Paw Paw". He was kind to all of the kids and often would give us candy and money to buy foot long chili dogs at the Five Points food stand on nights when we would stay with my grandmother whom we called (Maw-Maw).

Paw Paw did love to drink and hang out with other women, even though he was married to our Maw-Maw. But, that wasn't our problem we were just concerned about the goodies and treats that he would give us.

Well, one day at the age of 10 years old my grandfather asked me to come into the bathroom at the duplex that the family owned on Adams Street. He said he had something that he needed to show me. Well, he was my Paw-Paw and I had no reason to not trust him. My mother and dad were at work so we were alone. I followed him into the bathroom. He closed the door and began to kiss me using his tongue. He asked me to touch his private area, I pulled away, and he grabbed my hand and placed it there. I was so frightened and traumatized I was numb. I didn't know what was happening to me, nor did I know why my grandfather was doing this to me. Nothing further happened. I was so confused. He told me not to tell anyone that it would be a secret between us. I shook my head "yes" and left the scene as quickly as possible.

I cried silently that night and many nights thereafter. I wanted so bad to tell someone but didn't know who. I wasn't for sure if anyone would believe me. Who would believe me? I felt as though I had done something to allow this to happen but wasn't sure what? I felt bad, awful, unclean and disgusting. Now mind you, I never once blamed my grandfather, talked bad or thought bad about him. I continued to respect him and still thought of him as my "Paw Paw".

Life went on as if nothing had ever happened. My grandfather continued to accost me whenever he thought that it was safe to do so. He allowed his inappropriate behavior to permeate my mind, body and literally destroy my young being. And there was nothing that I could do about it. My self-esteem was gradually dropping. If I eventually did tell anyone, no one with the slightest chance would believe me, I thought.

Fast forward till I was 15 years old. I remember that one day my grandfather came to our house and asked my mother if he could teach me how to drive. I was so scared.

And of course, I didn't want to go with him, but I certainly couldn't tell my mother. So, I went with him, and soon as we got around the corner in the car, he started to grab my hand and tried to get me to pleasure him. I snatched my hand away and told him "No, no more. If you try to touch me again, I will tell someone about what's been going on"! He tried to offer me some money to smooth it over. I told him that I didn't want his money "I just want you to leave me alone". So, he drove me back home and never touched me ever again. After he left me, it was like a burden was lifted off me. I would see him at family gatherings but as I became older I never saw him again and really cared not to

Although it was too late, he had pretty much ruined my life. However, he didn't know what an impact his behavior had on my life and didn't seem to care. From what I understand he went on to accost other young girls within the family, however, they refuse to come forward. It was told to me that he became a deacon at a church towards the end of his life. God forgave him and so have I. Unfortunately, he passed away on September 17, 2005 and was laid to rest with my grandmother at Fort Logan National Cemetery, Denver, Colorado. God rest his soul.

"If you hear a voice within you say you cannot paint, then by all means paint, and that voice will be silenced."

- Vincent Van Gogh

College days are here again!

Now one of the most exciting times in my life was when I attended the University of the Pacific, Conservatory of Music in Stockton, California in 1980.

Prior to being accepted into the University of the Pacific, I had applied and auditioned at the University of Southern California. Now, just to back up a little I had no idea of how I would be going to college. My mother was a single parent of 5 children. I was the oldest and the first to consider going to college. I knew I wanted to go to college. I kept my grades above a 3.5 grade average, and participated in the Drama and Music

Program throughout high school. I took the ACT, SAT tests and filled out a number of college applications. I had no earthly idea of how I was going to pay for college, but I knew it was what I wanted and nothing was going to stop me.

So, I had an audition at the University of the Pacific. I sang "Ave Maria" in Latin in my contralto voice. They asked me "Who encouraged you to sing this song? Do you know that this is a very difficult song and we have never had anyone audition with this song?" I informed them that I had made the decision, because I have always wanted to sing this song. So, I left the audition feeling indifferent and unsure.

The following week or so, I received a letter from the University of Southern California to audition. Three days prior to my going to Los Angeles for my audition I developed a severe case of laryngitis. I could barely speak, never mind singing! My mother had gotten a bus ticket for me and set things up for me to stay with my Aunt for a couple of days while there. I was really upset that I could barely sing, but I went anyway.

My aunt took me to the audition, I did not do well. I was able to push the vocals out but it sounded as though I was pushing. So, I left and went back home. I heard from the University of the Pacific, Conservatory of Music informing me that I had been accepted into the Bachelor of Music Vocal Performance Degree Program. I was happy about this news, but, I waited patiently to hear from University of Southern California. I received a letter from them informing me that I was accepted into the University but not into the Bachelor of Music Program. They were accepting me into the Bachelor of Arts Degree Program, majoring in Dramatics. I was a little disappointed with this news for I really wanted to study Vocal Music and I wanted to do it at U.S.C. So I decided to accept the University of the Pacific's Conservatory of Music Degree Program.

It was so different for me being away from home and quite challenging to say the least. This was my first time on my own, away from home no one to guide me and when. Other then of course my class schedules and the rules of the dorm director.

So now, I would be at a college on campus, away from the chaos, emotional and physical abuse. Dear Lord God, You have saved your child, Far away from the feeling of being unloved, and unwanted. I felt free! However, even though I felt free, I did not feel completely free. There was still something there that was not completely right. I did not feel completely whole.

I remember attending my freshman orientation at the University and I had stayed overnight. Because I was still not completely whole and had not set up my foundation nor did I know how, I was promiscuous and allowed one of the football players to lure me into sleeping with him. I was young, fresh out of high school and naïve. I did not have a darn clue as to what was happening to me. Again it felt similar to the time when I was molested by my grandfather and just as bad, because I had promised myself that I would never place myself in that type of predicament again. Yet here I was. At the time I didn't know that he was a football player and I know that is not the point. The point was that I had slept with a strange young man that I had met for the first time, and unfortunately he would not be the last. It is interesting to note that this young man was drafted by the NFL.

Although, I had no guidance and support in how to handle the ups and downs of life I begin to delve back into my depression again. I had no one to call and was pretty much out there on my own. So, it was no wonder I was seeking promiscuous activities. I assumed that it was appropriate. No one told me otherwise. And my engaging partners certainly were not going to advise me, that is for sure. However, I refuse to blame anyone for my indiscretions. I took full responsibility then and I take it now.

The first year of my second semester of college I received a call that my grandmother (Maw Maw) had passed away as previously noted. I was truly devastated and unsure of which direction to go in. But, I knew that I needed to move forward. I knew that she would have wanted that and she would have been so proud of me. So, that is what I did. I moved onward.

Several months later, one of my favorite uncles died. He was my grandmother's youngest son. Apparently, he was shot by a woman and died in the hospital from his injuries. This was another traumatic blow to the family and to me. I was beginning to wonder if it was meant for me to go to college. That maybe I needed to return home and help the family? But, I decided that I needed to move on and I did.

During my time frame at the university I had many encounters. Many of them were unsuccessful and frugal. Well most of them were. There were a few that were somewhat meaningful and the young men really wanted a true relationship with me. But, because of my brokenness it was impossible. I would just push them away. I wasn't ready for anything close to that or any relationship at all to be truthful. I was looking for a true love and didn't realize it when it was staring me in my face. I couldn't realize that every man I met did not just want me physically. And there were several that told me so. But, I figured that if they didn't want me for that there truly must be something wrong with me and I ultimately pushed them away.

My studies seemed to be moving along at a snail's pace and I wasn't doing well academically at all. I could not seem to keep up and stayed up most nights popping "No Doz", drinking coffee and eating ramen noodles. The extra studying helped my grades a little but not much.

There were times when I would pull an all-nighter and study music history notes until I passed out. However, on occasion to get into the campus life style I would attend fraternity and sorority parties. Again, I wasn't up on the fraternity, sorority kind of life. I was just following a few friends and checking things out. One night I attended an Omega Psi Phi Fraternity party and I met a man there that again changed my life. You noticed how it seemed to always be men that make a great impact on my life good or bad?

The man that I am speaking of caused me to develop a fatal attraction to him. There truly was no real love for him, because I didn't know what real love was all about. I would meet with this man ever so often. It was a relationship that was more brief sexual encounters than love, however, I thought otherwise and that became the problem. I developed a true fatal attraction to this man and almost ended up in jail. I totally could not get my mind around the fact that I could and would never have this man. He would never be my boyfriend, husband, father of my children, nothing. Why was it so difficult for me to understand that? Why could I not wrap my mind around that?

I at one point became pregnant and thought that this would seal the deal on our relationship. However, it did quite the opposite. We had several talks about my keeping the baby, but in the end it was decided that keeping the baby would not be an option. We went out of town to a clinic. It was one of the longest drives that I have ever taken in my life.

Afterwards, my life became even worse emotionally. I became more obsessed with him and started doing strange things that were certainly not considered sane by any stretch of the imagination. But I was not aware of it at the time. It seemed quite normal to me. I began to call him consistently and often. He would only answer periodically. I refused to take "no" for an answer. It took me so long to get over the infatuation that I had for this man. Eventually, over many years I was able to get past him, but by that time I was emotionally damaged and too tired to care anymore, but by this time, enough damage has been done; I aborted pregnancy for this man!

My stay at the university pretty much ended after about 3 ½ years, right before I was to graduate. Due to monies being removed from my financial account for plane tickets during the time of my grandmother's passing and never being replaced, I was not allowed to return to my classes. This was in the winter of 1983. I was so devastated that I just didn't know what to do. At that time, I had to move back into my mom's house and was even more depressed.

I knew that I would not be able to stay home with my mom for long. I had worked so hard on developing my independence that I knew that it was going to be hard for me to adapt. In the meantime, there were a number of rehabilitative measures that were taken once I returned home. I was sent to Albuquerque, New Mexico to stay with my dad and his new family. I met my step mother, biological brother, sister and 2 step brothers. This I knew was going to be another challenging journey, as I had not lived with my dad since I was 15 years old. Time had not changed dad's addictive behavior. Some of his behaviors brought back memories from the past that I preferred not to be subjected to and did not know how to voice my discord to my dad. My step mother Lavana and I cooked and talked often. We were more like sisters and confided in one another in that manner.

I enjoyed my stay with my new family and there were some rough patches, but, I knew that I needed to be doing something more constructive. So, I decided to register for the United States Naval Reserve.

I went to basic training in Orlando, Florida and experienced another shock in my life. I was not accustomed to being yelled at in that manner again, consistently, day in and day out. It was most certainly a challenge and I stayed in trouble often about my cluttered locker! But, I was given the honor of singing at graduation! No one from my family of course attended my graduation, but I knew they wouldn't even though I had advised them a month or so ahead of time.

After basic training, I was transferred to Great Lakes, Illinois. There I attended the Naval Hospital Corps

School. It was a great experience and a very cold one too! I made lots of friends there and we parted ways afterwards. I found out just recently that the school had closed in 2011.

Basically, the naval school made me feel most loved at this stage, minus the yelling; I was used to that in the younger parts of my life.

After the Naval Hospital Corps School, I requested to be sent back home to Stockton, California, where I was stationed at the Oakland Naval Hospital in Oakland, California. While being stationed at the hospital I met a doctor (an officer) who engaged me sexually. I at some point was unable to handle all that had happened to me over the years and up to this point in my life. I became severely depressed, suicidal and was diagnosed with multiple personality's disorder. At that point I was admitted into the mental health ward at the naval hospital. I was in the ward for about 2 months or more, after which I was given an honorable discharge and released.

Chapter 3

"Life can only be understood backwards; but it must be lived forwards"

–Soren Kierkegaard

Back to the scene of the crime..

So, again I returned back home with my mother where I was again sent away for more rehabilitation. This time I was sent back to Denver, Colorado to stay with my cousin.

Wow, right back to the scene of the crime. I hadn't been to Colorado since the age of 15 years old and here I was. I was quite indifferent of course about being there. But, I was prepared to meet whatever was to befall me head on.

Being in Denver really assisted me in growing up even more. I met my oldest son's biological father there. When I became pregnant I informed my boyfriend at the time of my pregnancy and he said it was all on me. So, without a doubt I knew that I wanted to have this baby. I knew that he was going to be someone very special to me. I felt there were no other options available. Abortion was no longer an option as I could not stand it.

Although this was not my first pregnancy, I was scared yet excited. The father of course was not involved, no surprise to me. I continued to work while being pregnant, until the doctor informed me that I had pregnancy induced hypertension. He informed me that I needed to go on bed rest immediately. I wasn't for sure of how serious the doctor's request was. Yet I told my supervisor at my job that the doctor had requested that I go on bed rest and that I would consider it within a week or so. About less than a week later, I woke up to an excruciating headache. I called the doctor's office and was told to go to the hospital at which time I would be admitted.

My aunt drove me to the hospital. As I was getting dressed for bed, I went into the restroom. At that time I sat down and began to literally see white spots in front of my eyes.

Apparently, I had fainted due to very low potassium and very high blood pressure. I woke up a couple of days later. I wasn't aware that I had been in a coma, because, when I awakened I tried to get out of the bed to go to the restroom and my legs collapsed underneath me. My doctor came in to advise me that I had been in an unconscious state for a few days. He further stated that it was touch and go for me and the baby. I panicked of course, because I became worried about my baby. He asked me if I wanted to have a C-section or natural child birth because the baby needed to be delivered now. I told him I would try natural child birth. I had a difficult delivery, but my son arrived 4lbs, 6 oz. 21 inches. The nurses had to immediately whisk him away to the

NICU. To my surprise they took a Polaroid picture of him and gave it to me.

My son's entrance was quite eventful and has allowed him to remain as such. He has endured life's lessons and remains strong, resilient and determined even now at the age of 27 years old.

I have so many different memories in my life that were significant. My life I find was met with many different events. I was more than encouraged to tell my story. I pray that telling my story would give insight to someone that may be going through similar situations.

After living in Colorado for a year and a half I decided to move to New Mexico with my father and family. I wasn't sure if this was a good move, but it ended up being such for a number of reasons: I met my husband in New Mexico; the birth of my last two sons Joshua and Jordan; I developed a deep and meaningful relationship with God. So, New Mexico, the Land of Enchantment has been a place of learning, and growing and I have certainly done much of that. Thank God.

During this last stay with my dad, I truly was able to learn more about who he was. He loved me; I do believe that to be true. But, I think with the alcohol addiction, depression, inability to forget the past and move on and low self-esteem, he was not able to love, genuinely. Eventually, I would prepare to move back out on my own again.

I met a young man who was a truck driver, and his father drove for the same trucking company as my father. My father knew the father, but did not know the son.

I remember asking God to bring me someone who could be genuine and love me for me! I was so tired of venturing into dead end relationships. I was just sick of it! So, in meeting and dating this young man (who is now my husband), I was very leery.

We dated for a year or so then became engaged. Prior to the marriage in May of 1992 I became pregnant with our first child together (mine and his second by previous relationships). Joshua was born when my husband was on the road. At the time, I didn't notice anything different about my son. He was absolutely adorable, as were all of my children.

Down through the years I began to notice a few concerning things regarding his behavior. But, it was nothing that was truly out of the ordinary. The one concern that I had was the fact that he was 4 years old when he completed potty training. I told my husband that for sure he would go to kindergarten in diapers. However, the day finally came when he ventured to the potty on his own.

Upon entering kindergarten, I received a call from his teacher regarding his behavior in class. She informed me he was extremely agitated, would pull posters off walls, tip over desks and hide under his desk. I wasn't for sure what this was all about, but I promised my husband and I would talk with my son about it. We did, talk with him and don't think that he really understood what we were saying. However, the next week the same thing happened. So, one of the social workers from the school called me and informed me over the phone, that they thought my son might be autistic. What the hell? The first thing I thought about was the movie "Rain man". The social worker stated that we would need to set up an IEP meeting. Of course, at that time I had no idea what an IEP meeting was but I figured it was pretty serious. To make a long story short, it didn't go well and by the time I left I was in tears and angry as hell. The meeting included between 8 to 10 persons that included: educators, social workers, therapists and psychologists. These people talked at me from so many different directions about my child that I was becoming defensive. However, I held my peace, listened and took it all in.

When my husband returned home I told him about the meeting. He was just as confused as I was if not more. I really felt so concerned about my husband because he had a look of despair in his eyes. I told him that I had a lot of work to do for my son and I needed to get busy. Although, this was all coming so fast I knew that I had to get it together and comprehend it for all of us!

So, I began to set up various appointments with neurologists, psychologists, psychiatrist, therapists and physicians. It was a trying time and I thought that I wouldn't survive it. In between all of the appointments and setting up my son in his new classroom, my son was still having severe meltdowns daily. Despite no other alternatives at that time, my husband and I decided to have him placed on medication at the age of 5 years old. His violent and aggressive behavior was getting out of control and I wasn't sure of what the hell I was doing. God, are you really serious about this? Me?

We bought his first pair of glasses. He broke the glasses at least 5 times. Thank God that the optometrist was an understanding fellow. He was also obliging. There were a number of physicians that recommended that we consider placing my son in an inpatient setting, because of his aggressive and unpredictable behavior. I told them that would not be an option, period.

Fast forward through all of the meltdowns, IEP's, medications, therapists, doctor's, and lots of praying. In May of 2009, my son graduated and walked up to receive his high school diploma from Rio Rancho High School. We were all so proud of him. I was happy to be able to breathe again.

Our God, I found out has a peculiar way of doing things. In 1992, September of 1992 to be exact, I was not aware of how peculiar He was going to become.

The date of May 30, 1992 was an extremely special date for me. It was the day that I would marry my soul mate. This is the day I would get married to the man of my dreams. Preparation for the wedding was about three months ahead of time. I had decided that I wanted my sister-in-law's to be bridesmaids and I wanted my father to walk me down the aisle. Of course that should have been without question right? My mother and sister would be traveling down from California. I assumed that my father would be a part of my wedding. However, he stated that he didn't want to be in the wedding or attend the wedding. I asked him why, he stated it was due to the fact that my husband to be did not ask him for my hand in marriage. At the age of 28 years old, I didn't feel that was necessary, plus the fact my father and I haven't been that close. I figured that it was an excuse, so I just let it go, even though it did hurt. It was an excuse, and I didn't need my wedding ruined. However, a number of years afterwards, he attended one of my sisters, and my brother's wedding. I asked him did he think that he was being fair, he couldn't really answer me. Although, it hurt me for a long time, I had to move past it or it would kill me. I was certainly not a stranger to being disappointed or hurt, so, I moved forward.

We were married and had a garden wedding in my in-laws beautiful south valley home in Albuquerque, New Mexico. It was a wonderful ceremony and I was excited because my brother Jerol (J.J.) was willing to walk me down the aisle. He was so handsome and was my young brother. He looked trim in his suit as we smiled at each other while walking down the aisle.

In July of that year I also lost my maternal grandfather. I traveled to Stockton, California for the funeral service with my brother and sons. Despite the circumstances, it was an enjoyable ride. I hadn't spent any quality time with my brother in a long time. I had no idea that this would be the last time I would spend with my brother.

September 13th, 1992, I was sleeping and was quite restless. I could not seem to sleep. When I finally did drift off to sleep, I envisioned in a dream my brother telling me "I love you Big Sis, I have to go now". I woke up from my sleep, my heart beating fast! My husband asked me what was wrong. "Nothing, I just had a weird dream", I told him and went back to sleep.

The next day, I was getting my son ready for school. My mother called me and told me that they hadn't heard from my brother, and the military base was calling because he had not showed up for work. I told her I would come over later and just call me if she heard anything. So, as I was traveling back from dropping my son off at school, I received a call from my mom. She informed me to come to my brother's apartment that he had been in an accident. Upon driving up to the apartment that he shared with his girlfriend, I knew that something was not right. There were a number of police cars near the apartment where my brother lived and several police offers standing at the entrance of the apartment door. I knew that something horrible had happened. My heart felt as though it was about to jump out of my chest!

The police officer at the door asked me who I was in relation to Jerol L. Younger, Jr. I stated that I am his oldest sister. What's going on? Where is my brother? Upon walking in, they stood there and said "Your brother is dead. He has been the victim of a possible homicide". I dropped to the floor and screamed from the pain that I felt in my heart. I had never felt this type of pain. It was almost unbearable. My little brother was gone and would not be returning. I couldn't understand at the time why God would allow this to happen? It was almost incomprehensible. But as usual I had to put aside my grieving to be there for everyone else. However, as usual there would be no one there to comfort me. My newly married husband did not understand what was going on at the time. It was probably more than he could handle.

I was all over the place, being there for my mother, father and sisters. I do not know why I never thought of taking care of myself. So, I put my grieving on hold and played the martyr.

On the day of the service I wasn't sure if I could even attend it. I felt as though I just wanted to die. It just wasn't real to me. I expected my brother to walk through the door and say "What's up"? I really believed that the body in the casket was a fake! I figured at that time that I had lost my darn mind! I didn't know if it (my mind) would be returning anytime soon.

Fast forward through investigations, more tears, family disruptions, stupidity and whatever. It was determined that my brother was murdered by two men that he knew. One of the assailants was the boyfriend of my brother's ex-wife. I prefer not to give details as to what happened, but apparently, it was all about money. As usual, money is the root of all evil. People lose their darned minds over money even to the point of killing or murdering someone.

Both men were convicted in September of 1995 of 1st degree murder, conspiracy and two counts of tampering with evidence. They were sentenced to life plus 12 years' imprisonment. Not enough time in my opinion, but no matter how long they would serve it would not bring my brother back. I felt that there were others that should have been convicted and served some time, but God will take care. My brother was gone. He was gone way too soon, R.I.P. J.J. Love, Big Sis.

During the time after my brother passed I became pregnant with our second son and had him on May 30, 1993. Our "Smiley" was another true asset to our growing family and a way in which I was able to handle the death of my brother, as I was able to focus on our new addition. With the arrival of our new bundle of joy we truly had our football team. He was a happy and content baby, and he remains that way today as an adult.

He enjoyed sports and played junior high and high school sports. He was even made captain of the team a couple of times. He also loved his older brother Joshua, and always helped and encouraged him. Currently he is engaged to a beautiful young woman in Arvada, Colorado and I am looking forward to their union and my grandchildren, particularly a granddaughter, but I will of course take whatever the Lord sees fit.

My husband's son, my step-son was a welcome part of my life. I was blessed to have 4 boys at the same time and loved every minute of it. Jonathan was rambunctious and studious. We worked in collaboration with his mother in raising him through a majority of his difficulties during his teenage and adult years.

So many tumultuous situations have happened in my life, but there have been pleasant ones also.

To God be the glory!

I repented to God, asking Him to forgive me for not trusting His decisions when he took my brother away. Actually, let me just put it out there I hated God and told Him so. Of course, He already knew what my reaction would be and I'm sure wasn't worried one bit. And of course, He knew that I would come back one way another, because I was His child, He created me and He knew all about me.

After the trial my life began to have some form of normalcy. So, we started attending church on Sunday's.

I was not really quite used to being involved in a church setting as an adults. So, this was all new to me. However, my wanting to sing was not new to me. I hadn't of course sung gospel music in a while since college. However, I was always willing to jump back into the melodious, gut wrenching sound of the old "100s".

My life finally took a 360 degree turn when I finally decided to surrender my life to Christ. I had been baptized as a child, so I didn't feel that I needed to get baptized again. Although I made this decision it was quite difficult to understand and would take me some time to become accustomed to it. I could tell that my life was taking a shift into another season. This was a season that I was certainly new to and swimming in unfamiliar waters. Being around so many other people and engaging in so many different activities within the church was new to me.

We started attending a church in Albuquerque, New Mexico. The church was multi-cultural, Bible based. The pastor of the church was dynamic, straightforward and taught strictly from the Bible, no holds barred. I learned and accomplished so many things while being a member of this church. I also grew by leaps and bounds spiritually, professionally and in my relationship with God.

I joined the music ministry right away and began singing with the Praise Team, various choirs and assisting with the Children's Choir. I spent a lot of time at the church serving in a number of ministries and I enjoyed every single minute of it. However, what I didn't realize was that God was truly expecting me to surrender to His will. Serving was truly nice and God asks that we serve, but surrendering to His will is much more important. I knew that I truly needed to dig deep within and find the true person that God had placed within me long ago. I was waiting on Him, but He was waiting on me to get going.

I began substituting at the new Christian school that the church had built next door. From substituting I ended up teaching. What a joy! I never thought that I would be teaching, but this was the journey that God had placed me on and I was willing to enter into it. I ended up teaching for 11 years off and on at the school. My tenure at the school ended when I became too ill and unable to handle 4 hours of working with the children. I knew that my time would soon come to an end. I just didn't expect for it to come so soon. I still to this day have a heart and compassion for working with the children a characteristic that I developed as a young child helping out with my younger siblings.

As I have stated before there were 5 of us and we were all normal, quiet children. We were typical children and loved to play outside with one another. Back then, it was typical to discipline children by spanking with belts, extension cords, and switches (tree limbs in which the punished are required to obtain for themselves). Not completing a chore, taking something without asking, etc. These were typical forms of discipline. However, these forms of discipline I felt were not appropriate.

In our house at my young age my father never really was the disciplinarian. I can probably count on one hand how many times I was disciplined by my father. However, my mother it seemed was angry and upset most of the time. Unfortunately, most of the time she was angry, she would take the anger out on me. She usually transferred aggression by seeing something wrong in whatever I did at the moment. I wasn't aware of the similarities in the abuse that she was receiving from my father, to the emotional and physical abuse that she turned on me! I was confused as to why she would get so angry with me. I really couldn't understand it.

There were times that it really seemed as though my mother literally hated me, even though, I'm sure that she didn't. I could see it in her eyes when she would spank me with one of the chosen weapons of discipline that she would decide. Sometimes the emotional discouragement would hurt so much more than the actual physical abuse.

I would pray so much for God to remove the hatred in my mother's heart against me. I just couldn't figure out why she seemed to dislike me so. I still am not sure to this day. The emotional discord seemed to be lingering on as I grew up.

I was unable to really figure out why my mother seemed to have a dislike for me until I became 50ish. Yes, it literally took me that long to determine that my mother's anger was not about me, but, about her and her past life.

I felt that my mother was not comfortable or able to develop a close mother-daughter relationship. I dreamed daily as to if and when I would be able to get out of this world of emotional pain. I literally just wanted to get out! It was more than I wanted and I just didn't know how long I would be able to make it!

As I started at the beginning of this book, my sole purpose is not to hurt or harm anyone. This is my story, my journey and these things happened and I was able to survive and endure. I had no one to fall back on. No one to support me when I was down. I made this journey all by myself and survived it all from the beginning to the end. None of it was easy. But, I thank God for His amazing grace and mercy. There were so many days that I would go to my secret hideaway, close the door and cry so very quietly.

I'm not sure if anyone was aware of the medical and emotional problems I was going through. I'm not even sure that I understood until the age of 50 years old. Everything seemed to be unclear prior to that.

I began to have an enormous amount of sad days after the molestation. Depression was setting in, and no one knew, nor seemed to notice. I began to go deep within my thoughts and mind. I didn't want anyone to be a part of my thoughts and kept others out as best I was able to. I was able to close my mind off and find that special place that made me feel special, loved and beautiful. I had never felt special or beautiful prior to this. There were many instances in which I envisioned myself as a beautiful starlet or performer loved by all.

I began to realize that I was going into my safe world, because it was safer for me to be there. I had created my own safety net and it felt comfortable. But what I didn't realize was that God had already taken care of that for me with His Son Jesus a long time ago. I do thank Jesus for His sacrifice and there is no one like Him. However, like I stated earlier I was truly unaware of the implications of what being safe in His arms really meant. However, I knew that I soon would learn, but I didn't know what an impact our Lord and Savior would have on my life.

Deep Down.....

At the age of 15 years old, I began to feel very sad. I began to have emotions that I had never felt before. I began to realize life at different levels. It was all happening before my 16th birthday. I spent more time alone, crying and sobbing out of control. I had no one to talk to and no one I felt would understand me. I felt that I truly had a sad existence. I hated my life and myself. Encouragement was never key in my family at all. No form of motivation whatsoever came from anyone, due to there being so much dysfunction. Again, I reiterate that my family means the world to me, but we had problems.

This book is my life the way that I see it. This is and was my life and I am releasing the burdens, heartache and pain that have plagued me for so many years off of my shoulders. This is my season to release all of the past issues that have plagued me for so many years, almost consuming me.

I cannot explain the inner demons that have dwelled within me for so long. But I do know that I am releasing them into to the atmosphere via this book.

My first encounter with recognizing my emotional instability was when the family lived in Denver, Colorado. I had my own make-shift room in the basement of the duplex we lived in. I was hurting so much from my insecurities that I remember going into the bathroom and trying to cut my wrists with a razor. It hurt too much so I didn't continue. Actually, it made me feel even worse and I began to venture deeper into that never ending hole, not sure if I'd be able to ever escape.

Being on Adams Street was frightening for me. I was never comfortable there. It seemed as though bad spirits ventured in and throughout the upper portion of the house and in the basement where my room was. I was really scared being in the basement, but I was glad to have my own room.

I contemplated suicide many times in that basement room, I have attempted it more times than I can remember, but would never go further with it. I hated myself so much I didn't think that I deserved to live. I felt ugly, fat, stupid, nasty, gross, just a monster. I was unable to see the beauty in myself at all. And my family never made me feel that way by teasing and making fun of me.

There were many times when I would spend times in my room playing the album from "The Wiz". One of the greatest musicals I thought of all times in my life. Two of my favorite songs from the score were "Soon as I get home" and "Home". I have always wanted to sing and play the role of Dorothy. I would always sing those songs out of the depth of my soul, because the words spoke to my heart, especially in parallel to my life. I just wanted to find "home" and like Dorothy I was having a difficult time finding "home".

After a number of suicidal attempts while in college at the University I guess I was considered certifiable at the time. I was placed on anti-depressants, counseling, nothing seemed to really work. But I certainly tried everything to get me out of the funk I seemed to be in. Due to emotional instability, I eventually couldn't handle the overload and besides financial downfall, I emotionally fell apart and left or rather was not allowed to come back to classes. Hence, the downfall of Diana or so I thought. God of course had other plans.

As if my descent couldn't get any deeper, I had to return home to live with my mother. So, my slipping into depression became worse and I had no idea as to what I needed to do next. I knew that I needed to do something for living back at home was literally suffocating me and I needed a way out.

My mother and I of course were not getting along at all. She was consistently down grading and emotionally destroying me. I had no way of fighting back. I wanted to fight back, but I was frightened and fearful. Her words had cut so deep for so long I didn't dare test it.

I always wondered what it was about me that my mother, father and other family members disliked. Was it that I was so unattractive that they didn't feel as though I was worthy of loving? Did they think that I was so resilient that every awful, mean, rude word was just sliding off of me like oil to water? Did they think that the physical abuse I endured was okay and that the scars (emotionally and physically) would heal quickly and disappear never to appear again? Did they believe and hope that one day I would close my eyes during one of my many suicidal acts never to awaken again taking all of the family secrets with me? There were a number of times that I could have closed my eyes. However, I do truly believe that God had a plan for me. I believe that I was pre-destined by God to do great things! I wasn't sure when or where, but I began to figure out that He wanted and waited for me to make a decision. That decision had to be soon.

The evolutions of my emotional break downs were traced back to me, pretty much due to my being unhappy with myself. I was unhappy with the way I looked, felt, behaved everything about me was upsetting to me. Because of the way that I felt I believe that people could sense this and used it against me often.

Promiscuity was a part of my life as I searched for true love and someone to spend time with. Although, I didn't realize how valuable I was, men would date me for a length of time, but not often. I rarely had a boyfriend and was beginning to think that I would never be married. I figured that I would be alone for the rest of my life. God had a different outcome for me. Hence, my awesome spouse that I am married to now.

I have not always made the best decisions in my life. There are many things that I am truly not proud of. One of the things that I am not proud of is the time in which I was a dancer in a gentlemen's club. I walked into a club one evening because there was an advertisement for dancers. I really didn't know what kind of dancers that were needed until I walked in and there it was. Now the women were not allowed to strip down to the nude, they were required to wear tassels or stickers. I won 50 dollars from the first dance contest. However, I was naïve and didn't realize that it was a ploy to get me into the club. I'm not sure how long I was employed by the club, but it was one day too long. Being a dancer in the club was definitely a learning experience for me. It truly affected me emotionally. I could not possibly believe that I was actually doing this. I knew that I had lost my darn mind, because at the time I saw nothing wrong with what I was doing. And at the time no one was there to tell me otherwise.

What a complete mess my life was. I really needed support, but of course had none. It was all just like a merry-go-round and I just wanted to get off! This merry-go-round was making me so dizzy and sick. I felt that if I didn't jump off and get the help I needed I would possibly be hospitalized for a long time, I was just that sick mentally.

I didn't know who to turn to because I was so deep in my depression. I was tired of living, tired of existing. I came to the conclusion that I truly wanted out. I knew that the only way around that would be suicide. I'm not sure of when my first suicide as an adult was, but when I attempted it I shouldn't have wanted to do it again, but unfortunately I did. It was an overdose of Tylenol. In fact I practiced this method of taking myself out more than I care to mention. Each time I would be whisked to the ER, stomach pumped, syrup of Ipecac and charcoal given. I was crying out big time. But no one was listening and obviously neither was I.

You would think that after several suicidal attempts I would have learned, plus being placed inpatient each time for short periods of time was no picnic either.

I really truly didn't like me. I had allowed all of my past horrors to become my future horrors and they almost literally took me out.

One incident I specifically remember was when I became upset about a relationship in which I shouldn't have been involved in and that brought up past failed relationships. So, because of that and my emotional illness, depression, PTSD, and other things that were going on, I prepared to end my life that day.

I remember buying over-the-counter sleeping pills and alcohol. I remember taking most of the pills and drinking the alcohol. After taking the pills and alcohol I don't remember much else. I remember a friend of mine coming by, knocking on the door and trying to open it. I remember the ambulance and EMT workers talking to me, but not much else, after that. I remember being in the hospital and family members coming in to see me, but I couldn't speak to them as I was in and out of consciousness. The doctors and nurses would come in and talk to me and poke me with needles. I was unable to react or speak, although I wanted to. I eventually reacted to a needle poke. I was informed that I had been in an unconscious state for a few days. That was the first time that the suicide attempts had gotten that far out of control. God had given me a second chance.

After the hospital stay, I was transferred to an inpatient facility. Inpatient stays were nothing new for me. I had experienced a number of them due to my repeated attempts. Medication treatment, one-on-one counseling with a psychiatrist, group therapy, occupational therapy and other forms of therapy or activities as your doctor sees fit for you. Felt more like a rehabilitation facility.

What a sad existence for a young woman that only needed someone to love her and to care for her. That is all that she was wanting. Why could this simple act of humanity not happen for me?

At this point, many in my family began to come to the realization that I was mentally insane and would whisper each time that I would come into the room. Unfortunately, they really were not too far off from that insane part. Not that I was concerned about what my family said or thought, but it was what it was. Although everyone had come to their own conclusions no one was willing to encourage and guide.

As if I didn't have enough in my life, there was still many times in which I struggled to stay strong and sane! How difficult it was that whenever I experienced any type of encounter that I would become anxious, depressed and speak negativity about myself. If I was unable to accomplish, finish or complete any task I considered myself a failure and downward I would go. I told myself so many times that I was a failure that it has been literally embedded in my heart.

So many very different situations occurred in my life that I now own and don't blame anyone in particular. I just really wish that I had someone at that time to guide and lead me, someone to encourage me and to lift my spirits up when all seemed impossible, someone that I could just talk to and I mean seriously talk to that wouldn't take what we had discussed and turn it around to be a topic of discussion at the next girlfriends' party. I really needed someone because I did not know how, when, where and what to do. I just truly didn't know. I wanted someone to tell me. All I wanted was to know and I wanted someone to tell me. I needed a friend, a true one at that, a friend who listened to all my stories, mostly sad though.

I realize now that the façade that I perpetuated was just that false. No one had not a clue that I truly had concerns going on that were really serious. I ventured through life, merely existing. Although, I did have a fighting spirit, it would at times be knocked down by fear. My fear was of my mother, father numerous family members that were hurtful and unjust with their words and actions. The pains that I felt were just never comforted or smoothed over. Of course, I knew that they wouldn't be, so I just needed to get past that type of thinking. I needed to come to the realization that there was no one that cared or that was concerned.

It is required for me that I needed to stand upon my own two feet, put on my "big girl undies" and go get my life!

To face the reality of life, life can't always be a bed of roses. The major thing I learned during my hard times.

It is often said that tough times last, but tough people don't. This statement is, in fact, not a fallacy. Perseverance was the key to my being here today, in spite of all that happened in the past, being able to write this regardless of wherever I came from takes a lot.

Another thing in life is, in anything that happens, expect criticisms and discouragements, avoid them, and use them as stepping stones. Though I was left discouraged by the series of events that happened around me, I channeled them into motivation and used them as a stepping stone to the next level. Despite the fact that a lot of challenges were faced, with the help of God and as well as my late brother J.J, who could have stayed longer, I was motivated.

> *"No one who achieves success does so without acknowledging the help of others. The wise and confident acknowledge this help with gratitude."*
>
> **-Alfred North Whitehead**

Post Acknowledgements

I know that I needed to go get my life and stop depending on others to give me accolades and recognition. I needed to encourage and give myself accolades. I needed to find a reason to assure myself that I am worthy and that I am someone important. I need to be true to myself and know that my story is important and that it needs to be told. Someone out here needs to hear it and understand it. Someone out here has lived a story similar to mine. It would be sad to know that there are others that have experienced depression, molestation, physical abuse, emotional abuse, degradation, mental illness, loneliness, loss of hope and my book would never have made it out there to give those individuals tools to handle their situations.

When I first considered writing this book more than 30 years ago, (yes, I have stopped and started often) I was so afraid of the lashing that I would receive from it that I would shy away each time. It was not until I met a special young woman online (Coach Precious Bivings) that encouraged me and assured me that I could do this and that it was imperative for my emotional healing and overall lifetime success that I needed to accomplish this for healing sake! This young woman is now my life coach and I so appreciate her!

Of course I have had other's that have encouraged me to venture forward: My mother, Ada V. Walker-Younger, love you mother, much more than you will ever know, you are truly the matriarch of this family and we would not have made it without you; to my father, Jerol L. Younger, Sr. although you were not in my life much, I love you and forgive you; special thanks to my little Sis, Kasandra for counseling me pro-bono; my Sisters LaDonna and Antonia love you both so much; Ms.

Laverne Dunn (thank you so much for the opportunities that you afforded me); Ms. Vanessa Irizarry (God bless you for listening to me rattle on); Ms. Debbie Johnson (TenderLove Community Center, thank you for your expertise, knowledge and allowing me to continue to be a part of TLCC); Ms. Marsha K. Hardeman(thank you for your expertise, allowing the late night text chats, your encouragement and concern); Ms. Lillian Harris (my dear friend); Ms. Marvina "Cooky" Levy (sister, friend, confidant, and many other personas all rolled into one, much love).

To my husband, Adrian, you are a giant among men. I'm not sure of too many men who would and could put up with me! You have devoted over 27 years to this union and the last 7 years have been extra difficult. Thank you, hon., I do truly love you, more than you will ever know.

To my sons, Jonathan, Jeremy, Joshua and Jordan thank you for loving your mom and tolerating her mood swings. As if you had any choice in the matter.

To my grand-children Michael, Jada Lynn, Javon, Zedekiah, Zerenity and Jody. I love you more than you will ever know. What joy you bring to me each day when I think about you! Just the thought of each one of you warms my heart. Grammy will always, always love you. You will always be a part of me and I thank God for creating you and allowing you to be in my life.

To my unborn child that I will never see or know, I know you're in my heart. You will always dwell there for the rest of my life. I do believe that you were the daughter that I wanted. I remember praying, asking God to not allow me to have a daughter earlier in my life, because I didn't want her to go through what I had gone through. You know what happens when you ask God. He will provide.

If I try to figure out what my importance is in this life I still question. What the heck am I here for? Let's see if I list the important things first I would have to say, being here for my husband, children and grandchildren. They are extremely important to me. Of course, my parents despite all the dysfunctionality that went on, I love them both dearly. All of my sisters and brothers mean the world to me. But, what is my purpose and who am I? I am the following: Woman of God, daughter, sister, wife, mother, grandmother, aunt, friend, pretend adopted mother to many Rio Rancho kiddos, lawyer, doctor, nurse, teacher, vocalist, author, entrepreneur, evangelist, public speaker, volunteer advocate, advocate of the disabled, seamstress, college student, board of director's secretary/treasurer and the list goes on. As I look over this list, I am realizing that I do have quite a bit of worth. Now that I lay it out it allows me to realize that I have a purpose and that I am the purpose! I want to share my purpose with all that are ready and willing to receive it. God has breadth into me a new life each and every day and every day I want to share the wealth that my God has afforded me. What wealth you ask? The wealth of compassion, forgiveness, love, mercy and the sharing of the word of God. God has truly blessed me. He has allowed me to be and exist for so many years and through so many trials and tribulations. He allows me to lean on Him when no one else will, that is exactly why I love Him so.

God was and has been with me all the way throughout my tumultuous life experience. Group therapy and individual therapies were at times useless. There were a number of therapist sessions whom I felt could care less. However, I did have one therapist that was truly caring and purposeful with me. However, I was unable to continue sessions due to finances. So I continue to venture throughout my life taking anti-depressants and living my daily life in awe.

So now, fast forward to where I am today. My illnesses are holding fast. Hypertension, recently diagnosed Pulmonary Hypertension, Sleep Apnea, Diabetes 2, Osteoarthritis, undiagnosed Hypoxemia, Atrial Flutter, Neuropathy, Chronic Pain Syndrome, Bi-Polar Disorder and a host of other diagnoses that I'm too tired to list!

Sometimes, I arise in the morning with severe pain, stiffness all over my body. Throughout the day, I keep myself motivated and move onward because of all the conditions.

My difficulties with my illnesses reared their ugly heads in 2007. I began to feel pain in my lower back and legs.

I learned at that time that I had osteoarthritis. I attempted to deal with my chronic pain for a while, for 5 years to be exact, before I decided that I needed to have surgery. I went through many different treatments prior to that, but knew that I could no longer deal with the pain. So, in June of 2012 I had a Lumbar Fusion w/Cages surgery performed. It has been a journey that has been out of this world, since then.

Currently I am on oxygen 24 hours a day, a CPAP machine with oxygen at night, I take 14-18 medicines a day and have been on this regiment for 3 years. I have been on walkers, canes and back braces. Although, I am on oxygen I continue to sing in my church with a variety of choirs and groups. I continue to volunteer my services with non-profit groups that assist women and children. I am a caretaker and watch after my adult son who has Autism.

God has been with me throughout all of the situations that I have ventured in my life. I know that it has been no one but Him. I thank Him for loving me so. I certainly wasn't worthy but He did see fit to bless me and granted favor over me and my life. From a little insignificant child from an insignificant background to someone who shares experiences through a book. He thought that I was worthy and I thank Him. Nobody but God could do for me those things that were done. I've been through hell and back again, several times. However, God has been there at every cost, even when I was right at deaths door. He made the decision that I deserved a second, third, fourth chance. I was one foot within the door. Why, did He pause it? Why did He stop it? What was it that He was expecting me to do? What does He have for me to accomplish? I know that He has something for me to do. I plan to do it and not give up. I will not quit.

I believe that this book, this story is what He has planned for me to do. This story as stated previously is not meant to hurt anyone or to cause anyone to be discouraged. This story was written to tell the world that there was once a little girl who was a dreamer and allowed her dreams to be squashed by circumstances and situations. She finally was able to realize that she needed to tell her story to another little girl, boy, teenage girl, teenage boy, woman and male. I do believe that my story will help someone and if it helps just one that's one person who hadn't received help prior to this.

"But they that wait upon the Lord shall renew their strength, they shall mount up with wings as eagles, they shall run, and not be weary; and they shall walk, and not faint". Isaiah 40:31 KJV

I do truly believe that my waiting for the opportune moment to write this book was now. That God placed it in my heart to tell the story now. That God brought an enthusiastic and fire cracker of a young woman into my life for this purpose (Coach Precious Bivings). My strength has been renewed more than I ever thought that it could ever be.

I feel as though I am flying on the wings of God's love as He is allowing me to fly high. My strength is giving me the ability to run and walk!!

I do sincerely pray that my story has enriched your life in some way. My life has been enriched by the lessons that I have learned from each circumstance. I thank God for each lesson learned. Good, bad or indifferent, all were worth the pain. If I had it to do all over again I would do it and not change a thing. It has made me the individual that I am now. I must truly say that I am a pretty fantastic woman. I do feel that I am home now. Resting and relaxing. Loving on me. Comfortable and confident in who I am. This is truly what home feels like and I never want to leave its comfort again.

God bless each and every one of you.

The End

www.ingramcontent.com/pod-product-compliance
Lightning Source LLC
Chambersburg PA
CBHW070517090426
42735CB00012B/2823